THE BOOK I NEVER HAD

Regain Your Power

2022 Edition

ROSE BUTTERFLY

From

CHEER PRODUCTIONS

Title: The Book I Never Had
ISBN: 978-0-6452271-1-6 (Digital online)
ISBN: 978-0-6452271-0-9 (Hardback)
Author: Rose Butterfly
Category: Non-fiction, Self-help Book

Cover design by: Cheer Productions

Disclaimer

Author's email: reach2rosebutterfly@gmail.com
Publisher's Website: cheerproductions.com.au

Even though, it's my inner journey that has propelled to write this book, I know I have been profoundly guided by an unexplainable and mysterious power.

Rose Butterfly

Dedicated to a seeker of clarity.

I recommend you read this….

There has always been something immense, unbound, and a selfless energy that has driven me to write this book.

It is the powerful purpose, that the book holds in its heart.

This book aims and breathes only one thing, 'to be a support to you in this tough time and guide you through.'

I am incredibly happy to put forth the second edition of THE BOOK I NEVER HAD, with a lot more inputs on how you can move on from a past, unhealthy or a broken relationship.

It is my desire that, whoever picks up this book, is thrown into a dimension of achievability.

You are able to outgrow all that you are battling with. You are no longer stuck in the midst of impossibilities, instead you now hold a thriving heart that is ready to plunge into a journey of wonderfulness.

In this book you will find a lot of approaches that could be adapted to various scenarios of life, and many have benefited from it.

Even though the book is being addressed to her, it is only done to make my writing and narration easy.

Apply it to yourself, whoever you are, by studying your situation.

You will experience a transformation, because this book is for all; all those who are stuck with a hurt ego, crying deep inside, unable to find an answer and is in search for a way.

In your desperation to find a quick resolution, do not flip through the pages, you may miss out something especially important.

So, read it slowly to recognize where you stand.

It will help you to come out from the countless struggles that you are experiencing at this time.

You could find a leap point, or it may take longer, but you will definitely get there.

Love,

Rose Butterfly

CONTENTS

First Steps

It is for you to accomplish an insight into where you truly are and where you desire to be. This knowledge is the foundation on which you move forward.

Do you want to move on?

You need to take a decision.

If you are someone who have become comfortable where you are, by holding on to the bits and crumbs you get from life and have been continuing to live on this manner for some time, but still complaining that you are not able to move on, you need to ask yourself what exactly are you doing?

What do you want?

We can only do and achieve what we really want because somewhere unknowingly we are always giving away our vibrations which are like signals to the universe to help you out. So, you could be indirectly communicating to the universe that I am okay to be where I am.

Unless you say that you are not fine to lead such a life and you are truly looking forward for a change and to give away the junk that you are keeping, you may not be able to take the correct steps.

What you may not be aware is the fact that you have not fully come in terms with the idea of moving on.

You may want to at some level, but you are still not there and therefore you are stuck. Here, you haven't yet understood where you are and what your heart is holding on to.

So, the big question to you again.

Do you want to move on?

If not, why?

Ask yourself, go deep to get that answer? What are you holding on to?

Is it a habit?

Fear?

Lack of confidence?

Address the real issues.

You cannot expect to move on if you are willing to stay stuck.

Your Understanding of the person
could be wrong.

Surprisingly possible.

There is nothing more peaceful than a non-confusing relationship.

It's simple, everything is clear, and you both know where to head to.

But there are some relationships where you feel there is so much love, strong friendships, still things unsaid.

You do feel the love, but something is missing. Sometimes it's confusing. But you still decide to stay in, hang in and wait.

Why?

Because you do have a lot of love for him, and you don't want to ask some inappropriate questions and make it awkward.

You have feelings for this person, and you do trust this person. Your understanding is that this person cannot betray or leave you. You have formed an understanding of this person with your experience and your thought process, accompanied by the great feeling that you have for him. Even if things do not work out, you still would want to stay in touch and be in a healthy friendship.

Now, I am going to step in right here. And break that bubble that you are floating on.

If you are operating in this relationship from a space of unknowing, not sure what is happening, then...

Your understanding about this person could be wrong.

You have chosen to hang in there based on your understanding about this person.

But have you gone wrong?

You wouldn't want to admit it because every time you think about it, you put your feelings right in between your interrogating thought process and your feelings towards this person, creating chaos and confusion in your mind.

As a result, it puts you right back to where you were, and in the very same state you begin to commence again.

Have you ever tried analysing about how many times you have attempted to confront what is going on in your life but have lost your way somewhere in between your gravitating feelings and the truth, ending up exactly in the same place that you are in now.

You are ending up in the same place and with an effectively same result over and over again.

Now, dear friends, believe it or not but our judgements and our understandings do go wrong. No matter how much we do not want to admit it, the fact is that we do make mistakes.

We unbelievably have the full capacity to go wrong about the closest people, the people we call love or the people we have high expectations from.

It is important for you to know how you are behaving towards this person and how that person is dealing with you. You need to have a clarity there. Do you feel you are kept hanging in somewhere without any direction? Then, you need to find an answer to that. You need to know who this person is and what his intentions are.

No matter how hard it sounds, and you may want to push aside this thought but I want to tell you that you could have misread this person.

You could have made a mistake; you could be travelling in a wasted path.

And this could keep you lost for a long time,

if you are not ready to accept it.

15

What does your feelings say?

Feelings give us direction and decision-making ability.

My feelings?......

I am in love. I like him. I have such a terrific time with him. I enjoy talking to him.

I feel so special, I feel energized, I feel so good.

And then? What feeling does it leave you with?

Confusion?

When talking about the feelings involved in a relationship, do not think about the momentary feelings that you celebrate with the person but the feeling that it leaves you with.

If there is

worry

unsettlement

confusion

sadness

rejection

inferiority

Understand that you are not with the right person.

Have you ever felt you have been insensitively left to hang in there?

Do you feel the unclarity, the missing of a strong real relationship?

Do you feel he is fooling around?

These are the feelings that you should pay attention to because these are genuine questions your intelligence is asking, and you may be pushing it aside.

But they are real tools and a big guide to help you.

If you have been going through such emotions but never actually dared to address it, its time; you need to talk to your lover boy.

Be clear.

If the person gives you an answer which has not put your mind to rest, then it's time to exit the show and move on.

You could ask him to get lost or put it out in a more dignified way, the results are the same.

Just that the former one is more dramatic.

So, it's up to you to go ahead and do it. So, just do it.

It would be one of the best things that you could do for yourself.

Missing that commitment Heart?

Know the why?

It is hard to admit that someone could be taking your love for granted when everything else about your relationship seems fine.

It is also hard to believe that your dearest someone could be scared of making a commitment. But does that mean you keep going without ever delving into it.

What is commitment?

Commitment is clarity, it is the voice that tells you to go ahead. If that has not happened to you or if your partner has not given that word to you, there's something missing.

Either one, or both of you are unable to see the other person in the bigger picture. Do not approach this as a problem; instead, consider this as a valuable information. Why?

Because when something is not in a desirable state, it will eventually push you to the right path.

Your partner could have issues to committing and that can be always addressed and worked out, and you could fill in the missing blanks.

But if all is ok and if still there is no progress, and if you are wondering where this relationship is heading to and if he has not said a yes, it means your partner has the answer. It is a no.

The communication that you are missing here is...

'I cannot hold your hand till the end of my life. This is what I feel at this point.'

He does not want to communicate these feelings to you in fear of the relationship breaking or hurting you. But that is the reality what's deep inside him and probably he has not been able to face it too, then how can he ever tell it to you.

This is where you think and take decisions for yourself. If you feel that a committed heart is missing in your life, you will have to drop it all and seek what is true.

You cannot lead a lie for a long time.

Somewhere you are going to break. If that brokenness is what you are dealing with, face it with clarity.

See your brokenness in clarity to understand what you have been through and where you are now.

If you are going to push away everything that wants to speak the truth to you, it will all trail back to you.

It's okay to have no future with someone but it's important to know that and to take the right decision.

So, don't be sad over someone who could not commit to you. Its neither their issue nor yours.

It's just that you have different paths, and you need to embrace that more acquiescently and gracefully.

Think & Evaluate

You are capable of it.

You are an intelligent being.

For a long time, I was under the impression that when it comes to a relationship, don't think with your brain, think with your heart.

Have you not heard it too?

I did that kind of a thinking for a long time. Now, when I look back, I feel my actions did not come out of a clear thinking. It came from a place of chaos, sadness, and despair.

I used to assume that I should be following what my heart says because its love, right?

'Listen to the voice of the heart when it comes to love , something like that kind of a principle.'

And then I was there , the place called...

the land of the lost.

And it so happens that we get so comfortable in this land. We live there as if we were born and brought up in that land, and we don't even want to get out even if it's the stickiest, saddest, dingiest place.

This miserable place then becomes your home.

It's not like you haven't thought of getting out. But getting out from something is such a difficult thought, so imagine actually doing it.

It's like learning a new software program, and who would want to go to the extent of actually putting that kind of effort? (This reference is only for likewise people, feel free to choose your own analogy)

We always want to believe that things will clear up on its own, it's a matter of time.

One day he will understand me and truly value me for who I am.

Please stop waiting for all these fancy things to happen.

Think about your situation. Think where you are. Think where you stand.

And evaluate.

Be like a smart genius person.

Evaluate from all angles. Evaluate left and right.

You are gifted with an intelligence; do you know why?

To use it.

If you don't, you are just wasting your time here on this planet.

A planet where you have come to enjoy life to its fullest, realizing your true potential.

Weigh out this person. Ask questions to yourself.

Get your response.

Is this person treating you right?

What kind of relationship are you in?

Do you see a future with this person?

Ask questions, ask bravely, and listen to your response.

Stop playing merry go round. Move forward.

How does he treat you?

An easy way to know where you stand.

Where do you stand in that person's life?

Don't know?

How does he treat you?

You do have an answer to this one. Don't you?

When you are with the person. Its heaven. Everything is so perfect.

Now let's get to the reality.

Has the person introduced you to his family and friends? If so, as what did he address you as? How did he behave with you while he was with his other important people?

Does he include you in his big plans?

When does he give you his time? Does he do that when he is not with his friends or family.

Is he secretive about you?

If you are feeling uncomfortable just by reading this, you know it.

You have understood my point.

If he is behaving like you are some alien species that he needs to hide and reveal only at the appropriate time. Don't believe that crap.

You are not with the right person. Because with the right person, there is no wrong time.

If he has not yet confirmed any relationship but puts you in the so-called special relationship/person category, just get the hell out of there.

DANGER. DANGER.

It's the most dangerous spot to be in.

It may sound very profound and nice but nope, don't be that special somebody.

Ask him to hunt for someone else who would like to sit with that title for the rest of their life (which I hope nobody should fall for).

So, if you identify yourself as a special person. Please quit that position joyfully.

Do not under value yourself.

You could be in a misconception.

So, what does this exactly mean in a relationship?

Every relationship as it moves forward, with time, it so happens that you forget yourself.

You forget that you are a person who has a defined personality, likes, dreams, aspirations, and beliefs.

Occasionally, the individuality that you own as a person merge with the person you are with, complimenting one another and growing beautifully together.

This is a magnificent state.

But most times this may not be what's happening, most people experience the diminishing of one's individuality, eventually disappearing completely, leaving behind some not very good feeling.

The concern arises because it does not make you happy, there is a conflict.

Some of you may feel lost, empty, and disconnected with your partner.

This could happen in marriages and really long relationships, where you forget the unique personality that you possess.

For some people, it may instigate strong beliefs of oneself, like you are not worthy of someone that you truly desire, or you begin to doubt your own worth as a partner.

You may continue to live this way without being aware because you may not exactly be able to point out what's missing.

A compromising life,

An unfulfilled expectation from your partner

Can lead yourself into a space of belief that you are only worthy of so much.

You live a life under-valuing yourself and calling quits to your aspirations and views.

This is not a rocket science to comprehend what's happening to you.

Just observing yourself by taking a step back like an outsider will give you a clear view of everything.

You will be able to understand if the journey that you are going through is something that is bringing you fulfillment.

Sometimes, it is just a matter of small amendments or a good communication that is all needed here.

But understanding where you truly are is the key to the path.

Impact on your personal life and growth.

Is he a good nourishment?

Have a good look at yourself in the mirror

(Well, you don't have to literally do it, if its inconvenient; you can just pause for a moment).

Take a deep breath. Then think, how do you truly feel?

Do you feel indifferent to yourself?

Do you recognize yourself?

Are you so immersed in a clueless relationship that you feel like an alien to yourself. It could be almost like, who is this person?

But it's you, the one that you have been with for a very long time. And also, the one you have been missing for some time now.

Do you know why this kind of unrecognizable, disconnected feeling arises?

It's because during this time that you were with the supposedly love of your life, the time stopped for you.

You never grew.

Nothing came into your life that made you richer as a person. This love in fact could have made you more of a shallow person rather than making you a better individual. You may think that you still moved on with life, trying to fix things, financial progress, job promotion, but you don't feel that inner growth.

The growth that I am referring to here is the one that makes you feel that you are adding on more to your life and its moving in the right direction, where you feel full and nourished.

In the right relationship you feel all of that. The real good feeling from deep within. It's not that romantic, over the top feeling.

It is a calm, composed, mature, confident, caring, sensitive, responsible feeling.

You feel as a person. You can relate to another person. And you grow from within. If this has not yet happened to you...

Step aside from your relationship for some time, to understand what is missing.

And give your life a chance to experience this growth.

Its more easier than you think.

And its possible.

Did anyone ever tell you, that it's easy to move on.

If no one did.

Here I am ,saying it to you.

Well, I can't really say that because I was stuck in a void for a very long time.

My point is do you want to be in the same boat and waste away every single day of your life?

Things around you change when you make that shift.

It's a surge that happens within you.

How?

It comes from an understanding and acceptance of what is truly happening around you. Most times we ignore it and go about, but you need to open your eyes, your heart, your senses, take a deep breath and feel it.

Now, one of the reasons I was stuck in that relationship was because in some way I thought that's how it was supposed to be.

I made that kind of judgment from what was happening around me. When I looked, I saw it with my friends, in family or in movies. The message that I understood about relationships from people around me was that, it takes time to move on, move forward.

And I replicated it.

You hear stories about heartbreaks and how they are supposed to be.

But recognize,

you are not here to live and set another example of a told tale, you are here to live yours.

So, it's easier to move on when you are in the wrong relationship. You do not have to be sulking and living in a moment forever.

You could begin by accepting that you have made a wrong choice.

You have been wrong in choosing that person.

Accept that people can be manipulative, even if it's the one you shared so much love with.

They can walk away; hurt you like you are nothing.

Maybe you are treated badly, it doesn't have to be physical, it can be an emotional torture but it's happening to you, and you are still sucking up to it.

You don't have to.

You can decide to put an end to it and start a fresh life.

If you don't accept what's happening, you go in the same path, in the same direction.

Only once you are ready to accept, you are able to realize, then all you need to do is, drop it. Like its nothing.

No more love, friendship, acquaintance, or any other name of that sort.

I left it.

Dropping it from high above. I don't even care where it landed.

Why? It was so meaningless.

41

Take a decision and keep it.

It's hard. But you got to do it.

At this point, you may be at a place where you want to get out of your sad relationship, trying your best, and while you are reading this you are 90 percent there.

At the edge of taking that big decision to end it all, to move on, to let go and start afresh,

there lies a 100 percent possibility of you making a 360-degree turn.

The moment you stop reading this book or is out of a similar strong-minded thought, you are back to the same life, you just continue like you never took that decision.

You go back to the same place after a phone call or a message from the person.

You are like a toy that is reset. And there you go.

All over again.

Why are you even reading all of this if you actually do not have any intention to stop what you are doing.

My question to you is, do you really, really want to get out from where you are?

Or has it become a habit for you,

that you now believe that you no longer have the power to do it.

Are you scared to live without your addiction?

Do you feel you will never be able to do it?

You will never be able to let go off that person?

All these are insecure feelings wired in your head.

You need to unplug it.

You need to shake up and help yourself.

Because,

No one can make that life changing decisions for you. You need to do it yourself.

Mark it bold in your heart.

YOUR LIFE, IN YOUR HANDS.

It's your decision.

No one is going to take that for you.

I know it's very hard to stand by your decision.

You will waver, you will change 100 times.

But you have to do it. And you can do it.

Sometimes, at this point where you are, it may be difficult. As we go further down the pages, there are a few things that will help you.

Remember, if you are loyal to your decision.

It will set you free.

Don't put your relationship in a pedestal.

It is a trick of the mind.

This could be the trump card that your mind is playing right now.

It's like a defence mechanism of the psyche to protect you from getting more hurt, by not letting you essentially face the reality of the situation.

If you want to hold onto it for a while its fine, meantime gather up the strength to face what's actually true.

Symptoms include

- You think your relationship is unique and no one can truly understand the special bond that the two of you share.

- You say it's complicated.

- You think it's the pushing and pulling of energies.

- You revert to the non-existing fact that he considers you very special and loves you in a special way.

47

- There is so much love, yet so much pain and you glorify this.
- The twin flame relationship concept (I might have to suffer a bit of backlash from the twin flame community for putting it here). It's not an attack on any concept. I am just helping people to move on.

Do not try to escape your reality by glorifying your relationship and living with it in an imaginary world.

Some people find so much of solace in doing this that they completely get immersed in it and are just lost.

You need to become aware of all that you are going through and dealing with; mentally, physically, and emotionally, and not uphold this nonsensical concept and cling on to it, just because you are afraid to let go.

Please understand your worth and value yourself.

Contribute yourself to the world in whatever way you can.

Be part of the society that you are living in.

Engage, live a life.

Do not be caught up in this whirlpool of struggling thoughts and emotions, just because you refuse to accept the reality.

It's a dangerous place to live and getting out requires effort.

Now, even if you have dragged yourself onto this point, one day you will get a release.

The day you begin to think, evaluate, understand, and reflect.

It could also be now. This very moment.

Justifications.

Another trick of the mind.

Whenever, you feel like taking a trip back to the connection and the person, you begin with a justification.

You think about your moments, and you begin to analyse everything in such a way that you want it to point to the likelihood of it being a unique relationship, situation or a few mere mistakes that took such a turn of events in your relationship. You are at the verge of giving it another chance.

Now, how tempted are you to pick that phone and get connected?

But you do know where it will lead you again.

If your justifications are leading you over and over again to the same path and you being ending up in the same place, there is no growth in your situation, right?

Do not excuse your justifications as a means to get to the person and continue to hold on to him despite everything being pretty much clear in your face.

There is no point.

If you still carry on, nothing will come out of it other than more hurt.

It is for you to take that decision and abide by it. It's not easy but you will find your way through.

You will, when you are responsive to an understanding of what's happening.

Be honest about your situation and have the openness to receive something better.

Honour and respect yourself freely.

There are numerous things around you that you could put your focus to than constraining yourself to a person that keeps you entrapped to execute a poor relationship.

Remember, justifications are the minds chatter to waver you.

Pay no attention.

Feel no Regret.

It's a regretful engagement.

After spending years with someone, the decision to part ways is a tough choice and an unpleasant chapter.

You could be struggling with your decisions, emotionally and physically toiling with it, or you may be at a stage where you have ended it and is feeling a mix of sentiments.

At a stage like this, you are left with your emotions and loneliness and its easy for regretful thoughts to creep in.

Regret is a way of looking at your past.

You revisit the bad decisions and moments and generate an ill-feeling about it, engaging in self-blaming.

Does this sound good?

Once again, going through the old days, encapsulating the feelings that you have already experienced and submerging into something that evidently collapses you.

What do you think about this process?

You may not be consciously aware of any of these, because you walk into those moments involuntarily, but what I am trying to do here is, get your attention to be conscious, to poke you to take that effort to know how your thoughts travel, where is it taking you and to be mindful where you are?

Whatever circumstance that you are in now, it's not very wise to approach it with regret.

It creates a lot of self-resentment which will not help you at this juncture.

This feeling may sneak in at various times, as you tend to revisit some aspects of your life. You then ascribe a feeling of regret to the things that you could have done, not done, the better measures you could have taken, and so many, so many things.

But again, remember whenever you set your thoughts on your past, you are stuck.

You are not living the moment that is given to you.

You may not realise how precious and invaluable this very moment or time is.

Even if you have chosen to move on, regret can keep you holding there for awfully long time. Even when your thoughts wander into an accomplishment of how you have moved on now, you may think of the days that you had suffered a bad relationship.

Observe it, but do not engage.

Regretful thoughts are an unconscious way of whiling away your otherwise precious time.

Keep a check on it.

You need to breathe into you the truth that,

You are where you are.

And you need to begin from this moment.

Stop feeling bad.

You are not insensitive.

Now here is something, that most of you are going to feel when you intend to put an end to a relationship.

You feel like the bad person.

The moment you stop it all with this person, there is a likelihood that you start to receive messages and phone calls from your Ex, and when you try to avoid it, it makes you feel like the insensitive person.

And the good person in you don't want to do it.

So, what happens next, you begin to feel bad, you start to think again about getting back and before you can think smartly about the whole scenario, you transit back into your old self and there you are.

Back again!

If you are of the assumption that you are going to handle this in the most matured way, the best way you can opt is to drop that person completely off from your life.

Now, it may not be possible for you, if you are not ready for it.

You cannot be in a place by actually not being there. You cannot force yourself to be there either, even if you, so desperately wanted it to.

So, you need a little time.

A time set aside in reflective thinking, where you try to gauge and understand what's happening in your life and take a decision.

Now you are good. There's no bad person here, nor the insensitive one.

You are addressing that person who is important to you and that person is your responsibility.

You do understand that I am talking about you, right?

If you don't keep that one person in the right manner, it's not going to be good for you and all the people around you.

To make this happen,

you need to be in the place.

The Place.

What is this?

This is a space and time in your life where the shift happens.

It need not be only in relationships; it can happen with regard to anything in life.

It's a realization moment but I am just attributing a physical sense to it. That's all.

It's important that you are here rather than pulling, pushing, and tearing yourself to quit on a relationship.

Most times, you may be criticized for living with someone for so long, you yourself might have thought as to why you can't get out of it.

You think about it a lot, but nothing happens,

you make decisions, nothing happens,

you feel you are moving on and still nothing happens.

That's because, the shift has not happened yet.

This is not something that you can hurriedly go into or force yourself, but you can achieve it, be there.

Reflective thinking, acceptance, are all steps towards this place.

As you read further you will find many things that you can try and help yourself.

It will all guide you to the place.

The place is a decision-making moment.

And the best part of this moment is that you are very peaceful here.

A place where you feel no regret, no vengeance. You are strong, smart and you can sense your presence.

It's not like the many a times decisions that you have made.

This time you know it. Remember the idea of dropping and walking away, that I had mentioned previously.

Here is the time and place when you drop like its nothing.

And you walk with your head held high.

10 minutes thought break.

Try it.

At any time, you are stressed, you are bombarded with thoughts.

Your work life or your personal life, if you are going through anxious times, you are filled with thoughts of all kinds.

Here, let's take the example of your relationship.

When you have a troubled, not happy, questionable relationship, your brain is constantly working trying to find for you answers and solutions and comfort and what not.

At every point when you are working, driving, waiting, eating, thoughts can constantly be there or come up suddenly and sometimes it's so overwhelming and continuous that it drains your energy.

You must have felt this kind of tiredness many times. Most often, you don't even realize that you are caught up in it.

You are so living with it.

These thoughts create empty, unhappy feelings.

But what can we do with these thoughts, because it's so difficult to stop them and most times it's like a relief, or a companion when it starts to appear, because it always begins with a simple thought and then rises up with dialogues, explanations, and drama.

It becomes your inseparable buddy.

If you are able to completely stop the chattering of the mind, well and good. But most times, you are so caught up that you realize it only after it has drained you.

Now here is a technique.

You don't have to leave your talking companion. Be aware when it arrives, and engage with it for a little time, and then say I don't have any more time for you, so goodbye.

You could give it a 10-minute timer, as in, know when such thoughts come into your mind, then in a conscious manner give an instruction to your brain that…

'I will be spending only 10 minutes or even less time with this person who has arrived.'

After a little talk, like you had decided, bring it to an abrupt ending when its time and move on, with whatever you are doing. You don't have to physically set an alarm or timer for this, it is just being consciously allowing something for a while and then stopping it.

It's like respecting that person who has come to have a chat with you. Listen for a while and after 10 minutes get back to whatever you are doing.

In case you are driving or doing other things that require your attention, don't give companionship to your thoughts.

What do you do?

Tell it, I will get back once I am free.

This is what you do at all such times and places, where you shouldn't be engaging in the thought, like in a meeting, with friends, or when you are with your child or spouse.

These thoughts always begin with a non-threatening casual chat, luring you into it and then it catches up.

You may be very tempted to push your thoughts aside, but you must have observed how it just comes back even before you realize.

This then becomes like a war.

Therefore, it is important that you don't go on a tiff with this chatter box, because then you are establishing a tense scenario and thereby creating a strong alter ego that may put up a fight with you to keep coming and staying on for a long time.

Pushing this aside becomes difficult.

So, time it out and have a control,

rather than it controlling you.

If I move Away, I can get him back.

Don't take this sad path.

This is a phenomenon that probably most of you have experienced many times in your life.

Or you get love advise on this aspect.

This is how it works; you are all in love and so committed and all so goody- goody but he never bothers about you. Never there. You so desperately want him to call you, text you. But he doesn't bother to do that.

You are desperate to know how he feels about you and then this happens.

Nothing.

He is never there the way how you want him to be, he plays all that tricks and keeps you at a distance.

Basically, he's buying time from you and never really is serious about you.

Now the moment you take a step back, he responds.

He calls you up or texts you.

Most love Gurus advise you to step away so that you can lure him back into your life, making him realize your importance and how precious you are etc.

This is a nonsense philosophy.

When you step back, you step back.

Not because you want him to come to you. It's a decision that you have taken for your own good because you have realized what exactly this person is doing with you. Don't cut off or avoid a relationship because you want him to come to you.

You realize you are actually pretending here, and the stepping away bit has not actually happened. So be firm, understand what you are doing and be strong.

Statutory warning

When you take a step back and decide to quit, he will come to you; you will be so tempted at his kind words.

But at this point, don't go running back.

Be strong where you are.

A right relationship is forged with both the involved feeling like champions, and it should not be established over another's weakness.

Regain Yourself.

Give time to grieve.

Here's you, you have finally put an end to that relationship which had been in your life for so long.

Now you know that you need to move on with your life.

So, people around help you, they make you meet new people, you try out new things but somewhere there is an empty feeling.

You feel this strong sense of loss that makes you wonder, if you should be getting back to the person or not, because it sure doesn't feel good.

Now does that mean it was the wrong decision to break up?

After breaking apart from a relationship, you should give yourself a solid good time to heal, to recover and regain yourself as a whole person.

If you do not reclaim into being a whole person, you are not going to be happy, and finding somebody can never bring the true happiness that you are seeking.

I call this regaining time, where you allow yourself to recover by letting yourself pass through the grieving phase and not trying to move out too quickly.

If you had a relationship where you realized this person was using you, ill-treating you, there is a lot of hurt feelings left behind and it takes time to come to terms with it.

Often you will ask yourself questions as to why this happened to you, you may blame yourself, you will feel low, but you need to arise from all these thoughts as you cannot live with them.

What happened, has happened.

No more wasting time on it.

To arrive at the place where you can think like this, you need time; therefore, even if others push you to do things, do so only when you are comfortable.

Be patient. Take time. May you be healed.

Engage in fulfilling activities.

That's definitely a good step.

You do not feel like doing anything or trying out anything new. You are not able to recollect anything that you liked, even if you do, you cannot think of putting your mind or your physical presence to it.

You forgot what you really liked, what your talents are. You just don't want to do anything, as nothing seems to interest you. people may suggest a lot of ideas, but there isn't a penny worth of energy left to grab.

All you want to do is just be by yourself and sulk.

That's fine.

You don't have to do things to help you move forward from a relationship. You do something when your heart feels like it.

In fact, the solitude that you experience can also help heal.

Pushing yourself too much does not bring you forward.

But if there is a tiny, teeny bit something that you like, do it.

It could be like trying out new hair styles. Looking into new fashion, watching movies that make you feel good, it could be a really small thing or what others even think as useless, but somehow you like it.

It may not bring anything out of it but you simply like it.

So, just go ahead and engage in it. May be after you engage with it for a while, you don't feel like doing it anymore, then you drop it and do what you feel like next.

I used to work on these apps that merged pics and created some art out of it. I liked it initially, then I got bored, but I ended up getting a job for posting some pics on social media. Then I dropped that too.

It's like stepping on anything that you even slightly enjoy and moving on.

Eventually you will find something that is really fulfilling.

I don't want to draw a path for you here.

I strongly believe

You should find yours by yourself.

I am stuck

Then, change your focus.

Right now, you could be struggling with a reality of being stuck in a place that you feel that no one can help you out from. It could be that you are not able to move on from the thought of a person, an experience you have had or the feeling of being broken and hurt.

Consistently experiencing the feeling of being stuck will only allow you to grow and flourish in that space. At this point it is very important that you change your focus to something else, even if you are able to do it only for a very short time. Change your focus into a different thought, an activity, or a person. Let a momentum take place in a different direction that will help you to gain more drive towards change.

A flow of energy, life and newness will eventually take away the feeling of being stuck or not being able to move from a certain part of life that you have been holding on to.

This might be a slow process, but the important aspect over here are two things.

One is to look at something that is different from what you have been observing.

And the second not to stop the tide of change, you got to keep adding on to it.

What is happening here is you are helping yourself to bounce back to life by a fresh supply of memories.

There could be times, you might want to just drown yourself in your bed and cry or you are just not able to go along. Such times instead of going back to the old memories, put focus on something else even if it is only for five minutes. Then again give it another five minutes. You could do anything in this small time, cook, draw, colour, sing, dance, etc. These 10 minutes should be a creative activity involvement and not watching something on TV or calling up a friend.

Though we may feel that it is much easier to switch on the TV and call or text a friend, it will not make any difference because those are escape methods and are not something that brings out the release of a new energy in you.

This kind of understanding is important than just being in a space and thinking you cannot come out.

Have you indulged enough?

Or are you still seeking answers?

Not all relationships, not all people are the same.

Sometimes, you are with someone for so long trying to get answers, to fix things and be loved the way you want.

But things aren't working.

So, you feel that maybe you should call this off and start new.

But you aren't able to do that too. You go on.

And you feel you are stuck.

Then there are people who try to move on, by being with a different person in their life, but are still caught up emotionally with their Ex.

They aren't able to get out.

There could be various ways how you are bound with someone, but somewhere you want to move on, but you are unable to.

You could have felt it numerous times that this is not right, but you still live everyday with it.

One of the reasons why this could be happening is because you may need to indulge in that relationship a little more.

You are not yet ready to give up, you the fighter want to know it.

Know the truth, blunt on your face.

So, to face the reality and the truth, you need to go into it a little more so that you can come face to face with whatever is truly happening to you.

Somewhere you haven't got all the answers, or it could be that you aren't accepting it, which is all causing you to lead a life that you are experiencing today.

Hence, even if you so frantically want to break things off, the best way you could let that happen in a smooth way is by being strong and going one step more into it.

What does, to indulge, truly mean?

Now, in the very relationship that you are, you go in and be present with an intention,

To understand this relationship better.

This intention is very important, to not get lost.

You must have not been able to grasp previously fully, where or what your relationship is, because maybe, you yourself had not given your 100 percent to it.

It could have been out of fear or because of lack of clarity.

So now, you try it out, keeping all your senses open, watching, observing, enquiring.

At this point, you definitely should get a better view of your life, the person, your relationship, what it actually means, what you are doing with your life, etc.

By being here, you are able to recognize that if this is something that you need to hold on to or let go. You could also come to realize what had gone wrong from your end, maybe you could try to rectify it.

The purpose is to bring more clarity to you. It helps.

Give it a chance to get a better picture, so that the decision making becomes easier.

Now without any fuss,

you will be able to move on.

Because now you have understood it all.

83

Acknowledge what you cannot.

It's a crucial factor to move on.

You don't have to put a brave front, be matured, and push yourself to move on.

When things don't happen your way, you will always come across people around advising you to be more brave.

In relationships too, you are expected to be brave, not the one to get hurt, be sad or cry over a heart break.

You may a little, but the expectations are that you move on with your life because your inner strength and smartness can conquer it all and make that happen.

But if you are someone who is not finding this easy, let it not be.

You don't have to move from point A to point B at a prescribed time frame.

It's a healing phase of the mind and it has its own mind, so, if you push yourself too hard, you may never feel okay.

You may never feel fully healed.

It will just lead you into a habit of pretending to be fine, so that you don't let others make any judgements of you.

You may want to hold on to pretending because you have seen that your EX has moved on so well and you don't want to be the one looking like a lost lamb.

Does this serve the actual purpose?

It will only delay you living your life.

Therefore, be open, be willing, to acknowledge everything that you can't and that you are not.

While you may think a lot of things about yourself during this separation time, do not get into conclusions and assign qualities to yourself.

What you are going through is a healing process, where you should be able to see and understand exactly where you stand.

By allowing to see the truth, you are preparing yourself to come out of what you have experienced. You should be able to understand it as something of the past or as something that is not relevant to you right now.

It could also be an important decision yet to be taken, but you are anxious and afraid to do it.

Whatever it is prepare yourself and have the courage to deal with it, even if you feel you are experiencing something that is very difficult or its revealing characteristics of you that you never knew about or you feel ashamed of.

Do not try to hide what you are feeling.

When you pretend, remember you are also pretending that what you are not truly feeling.

It will not take you to where you belong, instead hold you back in every aspect of life.

Not accepting where you truly are,

will not only keep you in a loop of an illusion of moving forward.

But will also restrain you from receiving life in its intended glory.

Face to Face

You need to face every bit of that pain, insecurities, and concerns that you are feeling right now and deal with it in the most appropriate manner.

That's the goal.

Giving In. Not giving in.

What to do?

You may be going through a lot of mixed feelings of which, the biggest one is temptation.

How do you deal with it?

When you pick up your phone, you want to reach out to him, you so desperately want to do it and then later you may end up feeling bad that you could not resist yourself.

You can approach this whole dilemma in a different way.

If you feel you want to make that call or message and you are not able to concentrate and do anything else. You should just go ahead and do that.

Like I have mentioned earlier, you go a little more into that relationship, to help you understand what was truly happening and why precisely the relationship did not work out.

.

However, giving that call may make you look like the desperate one; what you have to realise is that your agenda here is to actually get a solid assessment of the person, what was happening and how exactly does he treat you.

How worthy was it for you to think and brood over this person.

You need to be the observant one from now on and understand, how is he dealing with you?

Was it worth for you to think and brood over this person?

All this is for you to be able to see it by yourself again and hence be able to accept what was going on in your relationship.

Therefore, this process is for you to be able to observe by yourself and see once again, with full consciousness, what was going on in your relationship...

Only then can you let go.

So, when you are giving in, it should be for something better, to get a whole realistic picture.

And the not giving in should never be a struggle.

If it is, you know what to do, give in without a fuss, without making a big deal, gently accepting what is happening, so that you never ever have to battle over this again.

Remember, you are not the loser here, but the one running for the victory.

Don't be in a hurry.

It can take longer.

You thought that by now, you would have completely come out of all that chaotic junk, all that you had gone through and struggled with. But look at you.

You don't feel like the way you had imagined; you are still carrying a heavy heart and all the pains of a broken relationship.

It doesn't seem easy and doesn't seem like it's getting better. You are doing your best that you can, but the thoughts, memories and social media doesn't let you achieve what you want.

You are not alone in this path but that doesn't matter to you, right now you are desperate to get out of this jinxed feeling.

You want to feel good and fresh all over again.

The quickest way to accomplish this is, by not trying too hard.

There is no point.

Yes, there is absolutely no use of you attempting to fix yourself. It's not going to happen, as your fixing will only come about in its own sweet time.

Let your mind relax and know that it takes time.

Tell yourself that it is okay, it can take time.

You don't know when, but it will sure one day.

For some people it will take a really long time, but being hard on yourself, pushing yourself and totally going bizarre in your head is not the way.

When you are healed entirely from a broken relationship, you should be in alignment with your true self.

This is a decent time to spend with yourself, the person you may have overlooked for a long time.

So, get to know you, all over again and then start anew.

Everything will work out well for you.

Feel the tranquillity of your brokenness.

Engage and emerge.

Being broken can bring in chaos and disorder in your mind, in your daily life, as your day-to-day habitual living has got disturbed.

You are not able to associate with anything around anymore because there is a contradiction that has happened in your life.

Your surroundings remain the same,

but your situation has changed,

your feelings have changed,

your sentiment has changed.

So, adapting to this reality all of a sudden becomes infuriatingly difficult.

During this period of chaos, you may be trying to do everything you can to make things feel comfortable for you, or start something new, basically make life happening so that it does not feel like this any longer.

Amidst all this, there is another option you could take too, and that is by facing your brokenness

By befriending it,
Accepting it,
And going through it,

You will get to know the true nature of your brokenness.

It does require a lot of courage to face this feeling, but when you can, you should sit with it and truly feel the depth of it.

You will have to sit down with that every broken bit of you and recognize it and take upon the intention to be healed completely.

It involves putting, physical, emotional, and mental effort.

But by doing this, you have encompassed the strength and power to face it and recognize the very nature of your sorrow.

This will gently heal you, bring you into a calm place.

Letting that brokenness calm by itself is important, so that it doesn't rise up again and cause bitter feeling in your heart.

Make peace with that deep darkness in your heart,

so that you can shine again.

Crying over the Why's and How's.

How long?

Crying is a spontaneous response to a highly emotional feeling that you are going through. So, cry.

But after that think, think with your intelligence about how long do you intend to cry?

If you are past a certain point, the most intelligent thing that you can do is to move forward.

Whatever that has happened, if you feel you can genuinely do something about it which is for the good. Do it.

Else, don't waste your time.

My question to you is, what is your objective, by choosing this repetitive mode of going over and over again on something of the past.

Why are you trying to pull and stretch it to make it your present reality?

Why didn't he call me?

Why did he do that?

Did I make a mistake?

Am I good enough?

What if I had done this? Or done that?

So many things.

But the real question is, how long you want to be stuck there?

Do you want your entire life to stop at that moment for you?

If you are going to do it over and over again, it will become your habit. And once you make that your habit, it becomes an addiction.

Then you effortlessly slip into that state.

So, get out.

Get out from that place.

No more why's and how's and travelling into times that you should not re-live.

You are unnecessarily dragging your beautiful life into something that does not hold any meaning anymore.

You will need to make a conscious effort

to not go there,

If you have been living there, for a while.

Falling into the trap of temporary solutions.

Recognise it.

Temporary solutions could lead you to a lost path.

When you are hurriedly looking out for ways to come out of what you are feeling or suffering, you may be jumping into things. The decisions what you take may not come from clear thoughts.

As a result, you may get into unwanted situations creating more ill feelings.

This is the time you need to pause.

Take rest.

You need to take it slow and not opt for temporary solutions that will keep you away from coming into terms with what you are going through and facing it.

Is it important to face it?

Let us examine, if you don't, you may get into things that will give you only momentary joys. Eventually, somewhere deep down, you will always sense a feeling of missing and lostness.

That is why, it is very vital that you face your realities and understand your situation and feelings, it will help you derive smarter choices and take better decisions for yourself

It is easier to get into solutions that you think will make you feel better.

But when your mind is battling to recover, all that it needs may be some time, a little rest and not a distraction.

This will give the mind the willingness to assimilate it all.

Imagine, you had a fall and it hurt your leg really bad. Now you know you cannot move, and you need to take rest.

But instead, if you insist that the best way to go about to heal that leg is to play football, you may cause more damage to your already hurting leg.

It is the same way, not having a track of what exactly you are feeling, your emotions, your mental state and just going about and holding onto anything that comes your way rather than paying attention to your actual needs is not a healing process.

Again, nothing can be said as a no-no because every person is different. So, if you feel like, only if you strongly feel like (pay attention here) go with your feelings.

Only if you feel it is going to bring a smile.

Understand your true self.

It is ever changing.

There can never be a true version of yourself, that you can pinpoint and conclude as the true self because we are ever changing beings.

With all those ongoing experiences, altering perceptions, understandings, feelings, interactions, surroundings, and imaginations, we are in a process of continuous change.

So, perhaps we can conclude this much that because we are ever changing, we hold immense possibilities.

If we have that truth present consciously,

we should be changing for the better, for ourselves and for the people around us.

Now, when we are at a place of brokenness, it is not a feel-good place, and we may tend to feel a lot of negative emotions.

Does that mean, it is true and final, even if it feels like the end of the world?

It is exceedingly difficult to think differently, but this is where you need to understand, that this is not your true self.

Your true self is never to go into sulking and be unhappy.

Even at this very moment, if you are able to grasp that understanding, you can change your reality and your experience.

It is just that you need to believe and accept that you are meant to receive wonderful things.

What you are experiencing right now,

is not your entire reality.

Sit down, and indulge into a feeling, of the possibility of magnificent things coming your way.

That is your reality, and that is the moment that you need to look forward to.

Even though, you may be feeling abandoned, hurt, and lonely, these are not the feelings that you are going to live the rest of your life with.

The supreme intelligence of the Universe does not allow that.

So, feel that power in you.

Smile at the abundance that you are going to receive and be confident.

All experiences that you go through gives you a new perspective.

They are all for your learning,

to assist yourself and one another.

Do not be stuck with old habits.

Start creating new.

It is not easy to break a habit nor to start one.

After being in a relationship, to let that go, is like letting go off your whole life that you had been living.

The decision to let go off someone so quickly in such a short time may not be a practical thought, especially if that person was present in your life for a really long time and was part of your everyday.

Even if you have broken the relationship with the person, there might be a lot of aspects that has not changed and are still part of both your lives or may be just yours. You could be still living in the same country, same house, going to the same workplace, catching up with the same friends, etc.

Breaking off with someone is not just about breaking the relationship with that person.

It is also about breaking the continuity of an existing life pattern.

Stopping that momentum and creating a new one.

You have led a life partnering with someone.

Not having that now, demands a change of direction.

A new plan, a new system, a new approach in place.

It is important that your life after breakup, is forged with an understanding that you will be letting go off every way that you have led your life till yesterday or making substantial changes that feels fresh.

At times, even when the togetherness is no more, you may still want to cherish the good old habits.

So, with time, you think it is okay to keep in touch and be friends.

Do not try to find a reason to get back.

This will only cause harm.

It comes with a price of unwanted feelings, doubts, and emotions.

114

After a while it may seem that it is easy for the two of you to let go, forgive, look past and be connected again and be friends.

This is not something that you should experiment with.

Not may be always,

but you are still putting a great deal of possibility of new feelings or dilemmas.

Once you have decided that the person is just not the right one for you, you have got to stop that relationship and not continue any of 'whatsoever' is attached with it.

If he is somebody who was making a fool out of you, you must understand a good friendship will never work out in that.

Leave old habits for the dead and be alive.

You can live without him.

Yes.

An incredibly challenging task right now for me would be to install into your brains that you can live without him.

You may not want to hear it that directly, but that is the truth.

Have you ever known of a time when this person was not in your life.

And did you survive?

Therefore, you thinking, that it is not possible to move on in life without chatting or texting this person is a silly thought. Is it not?

You have lived a life and you still can.

This fear of what will happen if you end the relationship keeps you entwined.

Nevertheless, one day it will come to an end even if you are ready for it, or not. So, if someone is not exactly right for you, do yourself and the person a favour and end your dramatic relationship as soon as possible.

If you feel you are unable to, you are going through an extreme fear of losing this person.

117

Which is not healthy, and it indicates the fragility of your relationship.

There could be a number of issues you need to address.

Leaving it all and walking away may not be easy for you even when somewhere deep you know this is not working out and may wrap up any moment; but you still try your best to hold it all together.

Like I have mentioned earlier, diving more into this relationship could set you free as you understand more about your scenario.

You, arriving at a clarity on your situation is a crucial standpoint.

Dig deep to help yourself and never ever be under the impression that you are incapable of leading a happy life without this person.

This is not true, even if it is extremely hard for you to believe it right now.

When you regain yourself,

this kind of fear disappears.

Do not shy away from being strong.

You need it.

No one expects you to be strong, after a breakup.

Even when people around you repeatedly say that. The people around you are in a way more comfortable handling someone who is heartbroken than seeing someone being strong as it kind of creates a contradiction to an expected behaviour.

Sometimes when you are very sure, and you move out and you feel simply fine, others may not be ready for that. They may see you as someone pretending to put up an easy attitude.

You are being all okay and fine about the breakup is not what the person you were with expects you to behave either.

Taking a strong stance in a relationship can be tough.

If you are someone who is experiencing a breakup, you might want to be quiet and not very loud. You may not want to do a lot of things, as you may feel you are being observed by people around, your friends, your Ex, common friends, the social media network.

Too many eyes these days.

But being strong and moving on is a clear signal as to how well you have understood the breakup, the relationship you just had and your approach to look forward in life.

It clearly does not involve the other person and you need not worry about it.

What does this strength actually mean?

It is your inner power to move on, without any pretence, complaints, or judgements.

Being strong is not about being all out in social media and posting pictures of you having a good time with friends.

It is about feeling strong from within and living by it.

Now, if you are someone at the verge of ending a relationship, after realizing how bad it went, be strong in moving on.

Say what you have always wanted to say, be true to yourself and what you think. Do not shy away because that is not what was expected out of you or because that is not what the person thought you would ever say.

Be strong wherever you are.

Do not let the fear of judgement slip your life through cracks.

Fear.

Know it.

Fear. Something that can pop up anytime.

In a relationship, fear could arise in different forms and ways.

If you are with someone, and not exactly happy with how things are going; you could experience a lot of fear of losing this person.

You could worry about it but may not be willing to deal with what exactly you are facing.

There are all kind of fears; of addressing your problems, issues, lingering thoughts, doubts or about going ahead and ending a relationship.

And when you end one, you are scared of being caught up with a similar one.

Even in the seemingly good relationships, you experience fear.

The fear that what if, this relationship too does not last. What if it all comes to an end like a nightmare.

These kinds of thoughts can play in one's mind because of past experiences of unsuccessful relationships or friendships.

It is difficult not to bring past emotions or experiences into every new day that we live, but if we can do that, we will be away from fear and anxiety and would be in a better mental state to address whatever the day has to bring forth.

Let us take another circumstance, where you are at the mercy of someone, where every message or communication is so miserly delivered to you, your fear level could be a way higher than others.

This can make you lead a coward life, unable to perform and do justice to the person that you are. Even, getting across the street could be difficult for you as you are at the call and command of someone. That overwhelming feeling takes control of you.

Here, your grief has turned to fear, and you are walking around with a heavy heart and tearful eyes.

Whatever your fear has stemmed from,
none of these are good for you.

There should not be a place for fear in a good relationship. It should only have healthy discussions and plans. If at all any fear comes up, you should be able to share it with your partner.

Doesn't that sound good?

It is because that is the way it should be.

The moment you sense that unpleasant feeling around you, step up and address it, because if not, it will slowly begin to engulf you and then start taking control of you.

Have the faith in the ability to make decisions and choices over something better than what you are experiencing right now.

Start afresh or deal with the issues, that way you save time and also a lot of aches and discomfort in your life.

If you are living in any kind of fear, you need to address that and eliminate it.

Live less fearful and more fulfilling.

Do not follow the cliché path.

Be Creative.

There are always obvious paths in front of you,

the path that others want you to follow.

It is the same even in relationships.

Whether you are in one or you are out of one, there is always the norm that is expected out of you.

So, you are pushed to do the things that everybody does, and in a tough time like a separation, you are not at your best to stand up strong and say that this is not how you actually want your life to go about.

You may not be able to push aside advices because they are coming from successful candidates who think has the best decision-making abilities in life. Why?

You were not right with your choices earlier.

One flaw in your path, your love life, your career, then everybody takes charge of you to guide you into the path of the obvious where you lead an acceptable happy good life.

Now, here is where you have to be a little more stronger than you were.

It is important, what you do is,

what you really want.

Allowing yourself to be tossed this way and that way will bruise you.

It is okay if you want to just go ahead and may be listen to someone close to you, but at any moment, if you feel 'what am I doing?' you should stop.

You do not have to follow the path that everyone else does.

Feel free to try something new.

When you feel low

Snap out.

There could be days, many days when you feel really, really down.

These are times when you feel you do not have the liveliness to do anything.

These moods can cause a string of similar kind of temperaments for days.

Instead of being caught up in a low feeling and dragging yourself to live every day, get out of that box you are in.

When you feel you are at a low point, recognize that you are feeling not so good today, but you do not have to stay that way.

Realise that you do have choice.

Take rest if you can. At least close your eyes for 10 minutes. It will help you recuperate.

We tend to follow this feeling very diligently, as if we cannot break free from it.

Today if you are feeling sad, stop at that.

Now you have a choice in front of you.

131

To continue and immerse yourself in it for the rest of your day or create a different day for yourself.

Generally, you are able to recognize these moods from the very beginning of a day, so you have an entire day ahead of you to work it out, turning to feeling great, productive, and fulfilled.

You could read a book, do something that you like and the whole feeling changes.

It is up to you, how you choose to spend the rest of your day. Therefore, do not be caught up in these sad spirits that take away your precious moments from you.

If you are able to appreciate the gift of life that you have received, you will just snap out of it.

And each time you do it, it will get easier.

As a result, anytime you go to that mood,

you will know exactly how to fix it.

Dealing with anxiety and fear.

How?

Among the many feelings that you are facing right now could also be this duo.

Anxiety and Fear.

Something that scales up as the day goes by and that which leaves you restless, tied up and tiring.

Now think, as a person, you are constantly able to sense these feelings when you are around it.

This means you are able to be aware of it.

They may overlap, as in one follows another. At this stage, you are not able to calm yourself and bring in a clear thinking or sometimes even control the roller coaster of emotions that are coming out.

But just understanding and bringing your awareness to it,

allows you to take a step.

Therefore, recognizing it is especially important, and it is as well the first step.

Anxiety and fear usually build up because of not being able to see clearly.

Not having a clear idea of what you should be doing, what your priorities are, not being in the right path (where your natural inclinations are), your approach to something or a situation, your environment etc. , all can add to extreme anxiety and fear.

It is more like a warning signal that you receive to check on what is around and tackle it.

So, use it like a superpower to address things that may not be in the right place.

Every day, if you are able to sit 10 minutes with yourself, clearing your mind and understanding what to expect from the day, you will be much relaxed.

In relationships, these kinds of anxieties arise because of poor communication and not being in a correct relationship.

Therefore, evaluate where you are, its vital to think what your situation is and take brave decisions in retrospective of that.

Exercises, games, good friendships (that have a positive influence on you) are all few ways to reduce your fear and turning it into more positive energy.

Engage in some form of art or other creative tasks that you enjoy. Even if you think you really do not have any, there would be something that you like spending your time on.

Enhance your skills, bring out a little more in you and give a boost to yourself.

Come out of that fear and spread your wings.

Anger. Jealousy. Vengeance.

Uninstall these.

All though, all of them are different feelings, they evoke negative emotions, hence we have put them together.

You could be angry at what the person did,

Maybe feeling jealous at how things are working so great for him

Or you may just want justice, the universe to wreak vengeance on him.

It is natural to go through these feelings because you are hurting inside as a result of whatever situation you are in right now.

But none of these emotions make you feel any better. And constantly thinking about it only pulls you down.

How do you stay away from these restless thoughts?

It can be achieved, only by coming in terms with what you have faced.

Whatever it may be, understand it, you do not have to over analyse and find meanings and blames.

If you are able to accept it and realize it as something that took place in your life but does not define your entire life or your personality, you will gain the strength to not be trapped in these negative feelings.

In fact, you should not be engaging anymore with the thoughts of that person as it only eventually brings in these feelings.

It is particularly important that you understand where your mind is sailing.

You may believe it is fair enough for you to feel this, as you have been hurt so bad.

So, the vengeance and anger may be very strong.

But you do recognize that nothing good comes out of it for you.

At least by now you should stop associating yourself to that person, so that you can continue with your life.

All these feelings are like a trap, it will never let you live peacefully.

And the way to go about is not by getting in touch and being kind and courteous to the person.

It cannot fool your mind.

What you should be doing instead is taking that person completely off your life.

There is no need for you to reach to that person if such strong emotions are aroused in your heart.

The person, his life and all that is connected with him, has to be chucked out from your system.

Forward

The courage to leave the past behind.

The knowledge that wonderful things await me and to hold on to the strength, forged by my experiences.

From here on begins my new life.

Did you know that many have
overcome this?

You can too.

Heart aches, heart breaks and all the feelings associated with it is an experience that would have been faced by many in the history of humankind and many would have successfully managed to overcome it too.

So, as an observation, we can conclude that there would have been innumerable ancestors who would have accomplished this task of breaking out from a heart break to go beyond what happened with them and move on and lead a wonderful life.

Hence, it is not an impossible feat, even if at this moment you are finding it extraordinarily difficult.

Whatever you are facing, several have faced it,

lived it,

some struggled with it,

fought it,

and some found ways to come in terms with it and make choices.

Today, it is your turn, your turn to approach it in your own creative way.

You will find one hundred methods to adopt from the knowledgeable, you could understand and learn about it, you can put it together, adopt a few, but remember to listen to your intellect and take on what it tells.

If it is a voice that is leading you to a better life, you take that way.

If it is a voice putting you down and creating unhelpful reactions, then understand that, it is not the way.

The lesson that you need to take from the experiences of others is that, to let go and move on is an achievable reality.

If it has been possible for someone else, it is possible for me too.

If someone else has managed to find that happiness and peace.

I can find it too.

Try to take this upon as a challenge to overcome the ugly and lead a happy life.

First of all, be clear what you are expecting from your present state.

If its time you need, incorporate that.

If it is more of that relationship you need, get that.

Whatever you do, do consciously and bravely and with clarity.

Get into a more courageous spirit to take firm decisions based on your choices.

Have your own Mantra.

Be in charge.

Learning from what people recommend, from what you read and by observing around you, is an effective way to go about, but also is the understanding that every person is unique.

We may all experience a lot of similar circumstances and heart aches in life, which allow us to extend ourselves to relate to another person and their life story.

You may feel so connected that you may pretend like it's your own story or may try to attach with it and follow someone else's suggestions.

But remember your pain is your own.

And your story your own copyrighted version.

So, following somebody's advised path may not be always the right one for you.

What you are experiencing now, only you can grasp, even if there are people with similar experiences.

They may be able to guide you for a while, but not for too long. You will need to create your own way to get out of this.

You can take help from all around you but realize that the willingness to get out of it and start anew has to be from you.

When taking decisions and following a path, despite the contribution from the many that has experienced comparable situation like yours, you still have to recognise that, what you are going through right now is uniquely yours and nobody will be capable to give you a direction that can be solely for you,

that path you need to carve out.

There are various methods advised in the book that you can try but at the end of the day, have your own mantra.

From all that you have witnessed, analysed and what you are feeling, you need to determine your path.

It could be a combination of a lot of things of what people have told you, or you have come up with, but something that you have realised and have come to a conclusion at.

It requires your thinking, understanding and input.

So, make a way for yourself from your deepest emotions and situations that you are in now and what you think will be the best for you.

If that does not work, create a new one.

A new mantra.

Figuring out a way by yourself is a wonderful way of self-exploration, and you never know what wonderful things you may stumble upon in that journey.

So, take it on, with an adventurous spirit.

Why letting go is the right step for me?

Examine it.

One of the key elements required in letting go is in establishing an understanding of 'why to let go off it is the right step for me.'

Unless you recognize why you need to let go off the person or a situation that you are trapped in, you may not completely let go off whatever that it is. You may continue to remain in that space of someone wanting to let go and be free but not truly able to achieve it.

One cannot say, I let go, and assume that everything has moved away. It doesn't work that way. You know that because you feel the same negative roller coaster ride of energy the next day or a day after that.

Letting go happens after you have arrived at the understanding that this is the best step for me, and I am happy to take this step and it is so easy now to put that foot forward.

Often, we hear people talking about letting go, but to be able to let go, it is important that you know why it is the right step for you.

Why letting go is the right step for me? Examine that thought.

Unless you form an honest understanding of it, you cannot achieve it.

You may wonder as to how to get to that state.

There are two ways to approach it and we can look at both of those ways here.

Firstly, you can let go by examining and acknowledging the futility of how you have been living by not letting go off something.

Secondly, by realising that it is the only path left for you to take now.

Let us take the first approach by assessing your life. How has your life been lately?

At this stage that you are in today, this moment, reading this book, you may want to be free of a lot of negative thoughts or just want to start afresh and feel good but somehow you are not able to get to that motivated state.

You have been living with a certain approach, lifestyle, your way of thinking and habits, how has it served you? Whatever that you are holding on to, is it doing good for you?

Do you feel like to just put an end to all that and have a better life?

To let go, you need to form a full understanding of what you are doing now and what good is coming out of your actions or thoughts that is beneficial for you.

Sit down and think about how has life been for some time? Everything that you do and don't do every day, only because you are holding onto something.

This will help you to realise why letting go is right for you.

Now for those who are stuck with thoughts and unable to move on, the ones who are caught up in pain and stuck with the idea that you will never be able to let go. Understand that letting go is not a gigantic task but a simple step forward.

For example, imagine you were in a game and given a task to carry some water in your palm till a specific destination. Now, won't you carefully hold on and watch it till you arrive at the desired spot?

But once you arrive at the destination then what happens, you are happy that you made it and let the water flow off your hand like it never mattered to you, because now you don't care, you don't need it anymore.

Letting go happens in an equivalent manner, it just goes off like it does not matter anymore.

You will have to reach to that place of knowing that something that you are holding on to is not real anymore.

You need to sense that it is no longer relevant for me to hold on to it.

Think about it, if it has not been working for you, all those tiring thoughts over your head again and again and you trying out meaningless ways, all just failing and shattering you every time over and again, what do you do?

The only road that you can take now.

Is to let it go. And move on.

What is Self-Love?

How do I practice it?

Here, I would like to discuss one of the terms that we so often hear about.

It is used and overused so much that it could be highly possible that our brains could have reached a stagnant state where we are no longer able to actually process what is required.

Self-love is often proclaimed so much as one of the most important part of one's existence. But what does this mean and what should one do? How do you go about loving yourself?

In this world, we can find people with all kinds of life issues. It could be a few aspects that one does not like about oneself or bad memories, facts that make them despise themselves, lost love, hurtful feelings, or lack of motivation.

But the actual truth is that despite all of these, you still love yourself and that is why you are still on, and looking out for answers and asking the questions like how? And why?

So, what is missing?

The missing link here is that you may not know how to conduct yourself in the situation that you are in now.

Most times, at different situations or scenarios like dejection, brokenness, being anxious, being bullied or lost, we do not know what to do.

We do not know how to face them without being frantically lost.

What you need here is an insight, to approach your specific need intelligently and calmly.

When you find a way, your anxious mind is at rest.

When you are at rest you are in self-love.

So, seek that rest and peace of mind by understanding what you are truly seeking, what your problems are and how you can resolve them.

Pampering yourself, finding time to be with yourself and having fun and accepting who you truly are all different ideas that people may suggest you try out. And you should definitely give it a chance if you really want to do it.

But despite all that what you do to feel good, if you are still unable to find yourself in the right space, it means you are running.

If you are going to run, eventually you are going to be too tired.

To love yourself, you need to address your problems and conduct yourself by taking control of it.

You need to be the master of everything that is happening right now in your life.

If you are unable to do it yourself, seek help. Asking for help is a smart way to get a new thinking into your current situation.

When you feel that peace, you feel love abundantly.

That love reflects love for yourself and everything around you.

Could there be someone better?

In your heart. No.

Out there. Yes.

How difficult it is at this point to think that there could be someone else for you.

When you think about all the moments that you have been together with this person and a life that you have led, you may think that it will never be possible to have so much of an intense connection with another person.

It is true that you cannot have the same kind of relationship with another person,

but you could always have a different, better, and a more enjoyable life with someone.

It is possible.

You could find a more compatible individual and lead a happy life, where your both views and ideologies match, where you have more respect and admiration for one another.

This may not exactly be the thought that you want to be in right now and you may not be able to digest it either, you need not do it too.

It's just for you to believe and understand.

In your earlier relationship, you may have created several wonderful moments which are hard to let go and may now think of it as painful memories, as something that eventually did not turn into a meaningful one.

The fact is that you do not have to think that way.

Whatever you had with this person may have been beautiful, but right now it has not worked out for you.

So, you need to think about where you are at this very point.

You are not in that moment of a lovely time, but experiencing something different.

If you keep travelling back, you will not come in terms with your real situation.

You have to understand what has happened and what decisions have been made.

You cannot hold on to moments of the past, to keep you tangled today.

Be thankful for the wonderful experience that you have had with this person, but right now, you need to stay away from any further thoughts rising up in your heart about him.

The struggle that you are going through to keep or to let go, whatever you are at, should not be existing. You should be able to separate yourself from all of it.

It is in your full capacity to make that happen if you have the intention to be in such a place.

Let not your habitual life pull you back.

The personality that you possess along with your desires, your little quirks, needs its own perfect match.

Hand that job to the intelligence of the Universe, and you will find your way.

In marriage while in love with someone else.

Ever heard of it?

This is a complex and contradictory position to succumb into.

While you are celebrating your life partnership phase with a person who may be a wonderful partner and friend or may be the person is not what you had imagined, you heart is sinking in love for someone else. This could be someone from the past you may have had a relationship with or known as friends or could be someone you just met and got your vibes connected and you feel in sync.

What to do?

Firstly, know what you are feeling?

Is it real or just a moment of thought? Is it something else that you need attention to? Can you discuss it with your spouse?

Ideally, you should be able to. But unfortunately, not many are blessed with that kind of companionship, or we have not let our marriage partnership evolve that way.

So, in a scenario where you do not discuss , you will have to either work on your current life to know what it is that you desire out of the muddled-up situation that you are in at the moment.

164

If you had got into a marriage with someone while you had feelings for someone else, then you have not healed from a broken relationship, or some kind of healing is pending there that you need to look into. It could be letting go or forgiving yourself. It is an area that only you know what went wrong and therefore you certainly have the tool to fix it too.

If you feel the marriage that you are in is wrong, you need to think about it.

You will have to know what exactly is going on in your mind, what is the reality.

You need to have a conversation with the person you feel you are in love with and understand what future that relationship holds. Clear communication is very necessary because what you think may not be what precisely is happening and as a result, people so often are shocked to find out how things have been working out differently in each other's minds.

You need to have a conversation with your spouse.

When the knowing becomes clear, you gain a certain freedom in your mind. Freedom that you experience in your heart will eventually manifest in your world.

Everyone should have a free life to live with people they love than to live by force and compromise.

Marriage is a phenomenon where you celebrate life. If you are not doing that, you will have to think about what is wrong.

Sometimes, it may not be the other person that you are involved with has caused this upheaval in your marriage, it could be the lack of growth in your relationship with your spouse and your family as a whole.

Many may misunderstand this missing and so often turn their attention to another relationship because of the newness that it brings.

Only a clear communication and thinking can resolve your situation.

Whatever said, there could be all kind of problems in a married life, but what definitely should not be there is, lack of love.

Complicated Relationships...

leaves it complicated.

At this very moment, you have a fair good judgment of how or what your relationship is like.

You know all the complexities involved in it and the challenges that you face.

It is a reality that you cannot always search and land in a perfect, non-complicated partnership, sometimes you are right in the middle of a chaos.

If you are amidst a relationship that has a lot of uncertainties, you must work towards gaining a clarity on how to go about your situation.

You cannot be in it, get affected by the outcomes and not able to take any stance on it. You should have the faith to discuss it with your partner and arrive at a solution.

You cannot expect to move on in the same manner, be hurt, come down with your own conclusions and suffer as a result of unclarity.

You need to step up to a great degree, if you are in a difficult relationship.

You need to be firm and decide, if this is what you want, if not step aside.

Leaving a tricky relation to resolve itself, will not work out.

It will only generate more complexities and tensions.

You need to approach it intelligently and take a stand.

You should be able to turn your relationship to a fitter and healthy, free flowing one.

It should not have all those boulders and pits along.

So, how do you do that?

By recognizing what you want from this relationship.

And taking the necessary steps to sorting out the issues.

If this is not tackled, it will leave you unhappy.

You have an opportunity to either turn this into a healthy relationship or put an end to it.

If you are someone who is seeking a companionship, let it not be a complicated one.

Only a free-flowing journey of togetherness

can offer you the peace and happiness that you are seeking.

Trying to be that matured person,
when you are not yet ready.

Is an indication that you need some re-work.

After going through a breakup, you do not want to seem like the immature, silly, insecure person.

You may assume that if you show what you are truly going through, it will make you look like a failure.

Hence, you put up a fine face and pretend that you are moving on and doing great.

But what you could genuinely be feeling at this point may be grief and distress and a restlessness to reach to the person.

A Few of you may go ahead and call up the person to appear as though you are okay with things.

Now think for yourself here, is all of this necessary?

This kind of establishing to be someone who has a matured heart to successfully deal with situations, is this required?

Does this kind of an act bring out any value?

Are you able to analyse what you are going through?

Have you stopped to be with yourself and offer a companionship, to console and resolve your state.

Or are you jumping into things?

Its justifiable that you do not want to be the one to look like a fool or the loser.

But what price are you paying for it?

Is the price, a wounded heart forever?

Go over. What are you truly seeking?

What are you expecting out of all your actions, your methods?

Have you taken measures like an intelligent person or like a fool.

Come in terms with yourself that it's all right to be not okay, and sad and disappointed when you are heart broken.

These are the emotions that you are feeling, and you need to work it out.

You need to recover from it in a truthful and healthier manner.

That is what you should be doing.

You no longer have anything to do with that person or demonstrate anything to him.

You do not have to pretend to be that wonderful, matured person, who was able to conquer all.

Also, you do not have to extend a hand of friendship with the person.

Unless you pick a healthier alternative for your life, you may live more of a pretentious life than overcoming it.

Therefore, do not hesitate to show yourself to you, come in terms with your sentiments, to be in it and do not put up a fake version of yourself.

You do not have to do things that prove something else out of you, or to put you in a better light. Your life is your own journey, and you are accountable for it.

There is no shame in confronting the ugly face of your emotions.

Let it be and confront it.

It is the most straightforward and effortless path

that you can embrace for healing.

174

Go on till it is meaningless.

Till it is unimportant.

Every time, you stumble upon his pictures and his posts on social media, your heart skips a beat.

You incline yourself to the path of curiosity, that sets you in the direction of wanting to know more about what is happening in his life.

You become unstoppable and sets out to spend the rest of your time in understanding what these pictures and posts say about him and his feelings.

This functions like a sudden attack of the mind, that once it is on, you cannot focus on anything else but being fully in it and finding everything about him that is available to you through the internet.

You go to his FB page, his status, checks if he is online, etc.

Once you are done, you may end up feeling embarrassed and may pledge not to do it again, but soon find yourself into it once again.

Helplessly pulled into it every time and also ashamed, you realise that you are not able to control yourself.

Now here is the deal, do not force yourself to stop it.

Go ahead, and find out whatever you want to know.

Remember, not knowing keeps you in a very agitated state, unable to move forward.

It leaves you hanging in a nowhere place.

That is why you have this urge to know more.

So, instead of trying to stop yourself, move further and find out.

Do it all till your heart is content. Let your heart and brain not suffer a conflict and be torn apart.

Look deep into what you see, do not be uncomfortable, read between the lines, if you want to, engage in it, try to understand your own emotions.

Live them.

It is your own feeling, grasp and comprehend it.

Unless you become aware to what is happening in your life, you will not be able to help yourself.

You must know the truth.

Once you come into terms with reality, you will genuinely not want to engage in these activities.

Your curiosity no longer exists.

You just want to move forward as the person is of no relevance to you anymore.

Do you not want to reach at this stage?

Hence, until you are there, you need to go on till whatever it takes for you to understand.

Therefore, examine and be in it, be involved till you know it and once you know, it comes naturally to you to move away from all of this and lead your life.

Realisation is the key to unlock your path to freedom.

Love-filled thoughts about the person.

How to handle?

There are days when anger and vengeance settles down and it flows into love provoking thoughts about the person.

You may not be able to hold back but merely flow into these thoughts creating a little bit of happiness.

Actually, what it does is give you a kick to move on with the rest of the day.

In reality, you have been away from this person for a while and your life pattern has changed, you need a little bit of him, so right now, even engaging in thoughts about him will do.

It is kind of an after effect of an addiction that you had.

But as you are invoking more of your mind into the moments that you enjoyed with the person, you are once again delving into a space of being connected with him.

You may choose to continue these thoughts, but you will soon land into a feeling of missing him and consequently rises your desire to contact the person.

In short, it creates a chain of thoughts and actions.

So, what do you do with these love-filled thoughts?

At first instance you may feel like at least these are not harmful reflections, so there is no damage in thinking about him.

But later on, these very reflections drive you in to deep emotions.

The smart option would be to not entertain these thoughts, as it may lead you to take an action which may not be the right one.

Being aware of your thoughts and using the 10 minutes approach can be tried out here too.

Thoughts, good or bad catch upon like a fire. So, if you put it out sooner, the better.

You got to get the real picture into your system,

whether you are engaging in wonderful feelings about the person or unpleasant views, it does not matter.

None of them are good if you have decided to move on.

Social media love gestures.

What does it say?

When in love, who does not want to declare it to the world?

And don't you witness it time and again through the screen of social media.

How many times your eyes have stopped on a great pic of your friends, colleagues, or celebs, with their partner enjoying the glorious company of one another.

Picture perfect moments, celebrating each other, the love that shines in their eyes, gifts that go beyond words and declarations that are heart-stirring.

After seeing all of this, who would not take a moment to reflect on their own life?

You begin to evaluate and may feel a little sad that your partner does not display any such affection when he has an opportunity to do it.

No mind-blowing words, no gratitude to the universe for bringing you into his life, no gifts, no pictures of you that says you are the most beautiful one, when in reality you do not mind having a taste of all of this.

With the internet being filled with all these love gestures, it is easy to feel not enough and consistently feel that you are denied experiencing something so wonderful.

You may not want everything of that, but may be a little, may be a lot.

All those appreciating words, pictures, the moments, all create a missing out feel in your heart.

It is certainly an experience, to be appreciated and valued by the most important person in your life, and such display of love can bring in a great deal of boost to that relationship.

An interaction that you enjoy in public is sweet in its own way too, but it is not the entirety of a relationship.

You cannot weigh that alongside your relationship to evaluate the gravity that your love holds, it could be a wrong move.

These social deeds are merely a way of being with one another and nothing further than that.

It is not more or less of love.

You should not be considering it at all if you are in a sincere relationship, as you have your own agenda to plan ahead, and such trivialities should not matter.

You will have to go by the nature of the person you are with.

Most people are not comfortable or does not hold any value in such public display, as it may seem way too time consuming and pointless for them.

Some may feel conscious and shy about it.

In the long run, you cannot keep up with such gestures. Therefore, these things should take a back seat and you should focus more on both of you and that what matters.

A true love is much more than a few clicks.

Overcoming the feeling of dejection.

Tough Job.

Of all the emotions that you have been going through, the one that you do not directly address is the feeling of dejection.

All your anger, jealousy, anxiety, fear, have all stem from this very core.

It is the most hardest to deal with, or to ignore, and yet, never been able to confront; we always go around it.

We can cry about it but still not handle it.

Why?

It has destroyed some fundamental beliefs,

someone has changed your trust system; made you feel like you never matter anymore.

Once upon a time, when you had made that person your universe or your centre, you were going around it.

Now that the person does not want you, you have lost your balance.

You feel so little, like an invisible person.

Your ego has been crumpled so much, that you feel that there is no significance of you being, or not being in the world.

When you now view the world in relation to what you are currently experiencing, you may feel people ignoring you, you feel more timid, your voice not being heard.

The recovery of the crushed ego is a much slow and stiffer path.

So, instead of struggling and fighting to build up your lost self and your trampled spirit, let your ego rest.

You take this ego- break, by letting things as it is, and enjoying the beauty around you.

Take it slow, observing the tiniest of things and the wonderment it possess, all the things you have missed over the past few years.

It is a step of escaping and immersing at the same time.

You flee from the bondage of building a lost ego, and you indulge in the wonderment spirit of the universe.

No more looking around to build a broken you, because you have let go off that brokenness, you are not working on that project anymore but enjoying the mesmerizing world around you.

It is in this direction, that you will find peace, calmness, and alignment.

You no longer focus on how much of you have been hurt, and you discard all the past strings and feel afresh.

Can you become this new creation?

On contrary to attaching yourself to what has happened in the past, can you just focus on what has to be done today?

Can you observe your surroundings and see what your role is and take part in it.

Can you be the daughter and sons of this earth?

Are you able to grasp, how much more of a larger responsibility is on your shoulder, than looking at something that is gone by.

Do not hold your ego under someone's mercy.
Move on.

Do not dramatize.

Learn the new art.

Whenever we go through tough times, we may be forced to dramatize it.

It could be an unconscious outcome, as a result of what we have been exposed through books and movies, that we feel the need to behave in an exaggerated manner.

The front that we are putting out, may not be a thorough thought one.

We may be just acting in a manner that we are most used to seeing around.

Before you jump into conclusions and reactions, think about your situation.

There might not be a need to approach it with so much gravity like you are doing it right now.

You could deal with the same situation in a different method.

If you are ready to think a little harder, you may find your own unique way to cope with what is happening to you.

Realize that dramatizing is not a requirement.

Be free to cut off yourself from all the suffocating strings attached to a breakup. You do not have to be in it or do it that way.

When you stop performing similar to whatever you have been exposed to, you will realise that it is not so bad.

All that heaviness is created by you, because you thought that it had to be that way.

You put extra boulders on to an already sad state that you are going through. You then pack it up and put it on your back, so that you can sense it all the time.

Instead of adding more fuel, ease and take it in a more calm manner.

Approach it with grace and intelligence.

Think about what you can do, reason how you can handle this whole situation, rather than imitating the typical path of sorrow and misery and all the negativity that comes along with it. You do not have to execute everything in such a dramatic manner.

Be in charge of your own life.

Is all okay not okay with you?

Dealing with this unusual feeling.

Some days, you simply feel fine, like everything is okay, and the feel of a good energy around you.

You begin to sense like everything is going to work out well and that you are going to get out of all that mess that you have been experiencing lately.

You get this urge to begin all afresh.

But then suddenly, you think about how you are feeling.

You begin to analyse, why are you feeling okay.

You did not do anything in particular yesterday, to feel this way. It is almost like you do not trust this good feeling that you are experiencing at the moment.

You may feel like, am I really okay or is it just some temporary thing that is going to die away by the end of the day?

Would I be going back to that ill-feeling again?

Because how can I be okay?

Is it not too soon or sudden to feel this way?

Why am I feeling this way today?

It is so confusing right? When you are not okay, you want to feel better.

But on a day, you feel good, you are not able to accept that mood as you feel the need to continue in the most familiar feeling that you have been experiencing lately.

It is the reluctance of our brain to accept the unknown.

The reality is, your heart and mind is feeling fine today, and it is healing and preparing itself for it.

But you are not able to accept that, and hence you are confused, and you feel fearful and weird.

All this feeling is because you are in an unfamiliar territory, that is all.

Learn to accept the good that is coming around.

When you are going through a sad phase, it will be difficult to accept anything good that comes your way.

You will be unable to recognize it.

I want to shake you off from that momentum, and tell you to enjoy the good that comes your way, accept it.

It is yours, it is for you, you deserve it.

You are worthy of all that and much more.

Embrace and immerse in this good sensation. This is what you should be growing into every day, not the one you were familiar with.

Understand and believe that it is fine to feel fine, to move on and be happy.

Regaining Trust.

Slow and steady wins a heart.

After moving out from a relationship that has been through a lot of ups and downs, breaks, and patch-up, it is not an easy choice to go on that road again.

Even if you feel you have given yourself enough time, you may feel unsure or have a hesitancy to be with someone new.

Firstly,

It is important that you know where you are, and if you are ready for this.

At times, only when you step out, you realise you need more time.

Sometimes, you need to go a little further, and give someone a chance. And, if that ends up as the right decision, you will rise above your pain, and you will be able to appreciate the value of a secure companionship.

Occasionally,

Even if you have ended up with a great person, you may tend to experience some sort of distance from him, you may feel like the old memories are beckoning you.

In fact, some days, you may end up thinking more about your earlier relationship, and you may feel an urge to get back to him.

Be aware of what you are experiencing internally, what is the issue?

Maybe a talk and a good time with your current partner is what you are missing, and it is compensating by taking you down a memory lane with someone else, the times when you had a great rapport, and you begin to playback some good old together moments.

Or it could be some issue that you have still not addressed.

Else, it could be an impish, short time- travel of the mind that you should not be entertaining.

When you move into a new relationship, let it be slow and natural than a compelled one.

If you are finding it difficult to be romantically involved with someone you think is great, maybe you need a little more time and you should be open about what you are feeling.

A heart-to-heart talk where you both understand each other is the foundation of a good relationship.

Make sure that is the path you are taking.

If you are heavy hearted about trusting another person, due to issues you have had in the previous relationship, have an open conversation about it.

Remember, mind always tries to bring in old memories to play its ways, but the trick is to detach yourself from your past.

Be conscious and aware of the understanding that not all are same and so is relationships and experiences, they are different too. Therefore, reason with yourself and go in with confidence.

Absorb what life taught you,

but do not attach to the past when taking on a new path.

Thank You

Once again to the known and the unknown that has made this book come this far.

Thank you, my Love, for your support, time, your suggestions, and input.

All my family and friends, forever showering your love and blessings.

And my readers for believing in my work and your valuable feedback.

Share

If you think there is someone who might need this book, do not forget to recommend the book and be a guiding light.

Contribute

Write a review of the book on your preferred channel. Share what you thought was insightful and helpful from this book.

Get up and get creative

Share how the book made an impact. Send us your power art, a representation of that great feeling of energy. Express it through poems, art, music, acting, cooking, dancing, animation, comics.

We love it all, as we at Cheer are cheerful lovers of art from heart.

Be a part of the Cheer family.
Visit: www. cheerproductions.com.au

The Author

Rose Butterfly is an Indian Australian writer and publisher, known for The BOOK I NEVER HAD, published in 2020.

As someone who is more of a multipotentialite, she started off her career as a Radio Jockey for a morning drive time show in the United Arab Emirates and further explored her skills as a copywriter, marketing professional, author, and mentor.

She is also a theatre performer and an artist, and it is her love for creative expressions, entertainment and fun that drives her.

At present she is busy with her production house 'Cheer' which is on an expansion with a lot of upcoming projects.

She is the co-creator and editor of kids' books like the Turtle who could not tuck, Paper Plane, One Different farmer, Magic Plant, and many other children's books.

The second Edition of THE BOOK I NEVER HAD, has come out specifically to include some relevant topics that her readers have been asking her to write about.

Keen attention has been paid to incorporate it all. These topics and many other subjects will be further discussed through her blogs and on other media platforms.

Rose Butterfly is always happy to hear from her readers and enjoys that connection. So, don't hesitate to send us your regards, comments, or suggestions.

Visit the website to know more about the Author and other works.

www. rosebutterfly.com.au

Questions most frequently asked.

Answered.

How can I stop myself from unhealthy relationships?

Firstly, it is great that you are able to understand that you are putting your time somewhere that is not worthy. It is not easy to get to this stage. Most people are still stuck in believing it's okay, because they are unable to see how little time each one of us have here, on this planet.

Now, having realised that you are in unhealthy relationships, what should you do?

Firstly, try to remain in that understanding and not to be pulled back into your temptations.

Ask yourself questions as to what you are seeking. Are you trying to get past something?

Once you truly understand your value, you will know that you have got a whole lot of better things to do in this life. And then it becomes easy to not to go for something that takes away your precious time. You will observe that you are guided to more fulfilling paths as now you can see it.

How can I remain to be in a state of being motivated?

Do not confuse tiredness with lack of motivation. Sometimes you can experience low energy because you could be just exhausted. In times like this, you need good rest and sleep and maybe a break.

Now, in case you feel motivated one day but not another day, you need to check on this activity. Is it something that you really like, you want to do?

Recognise that, at times it is okay not to feel like doing your something, despite it being something that you totally love.

A change of a monotonous activity can bring about a kick of energy.

Again, if you are thinking of motivation as a state of being in a good mood, you will need to understand your life circumstances and if there is anything that is upsetting you beyond a point where it is killing your happiness.

Ideally you should be in a state of happiness deep inside, doing what you love should motivate you and a good rest should keep you going.

207

What is the meaning of seeing synchronised numbers like 1111 or 2222?

When you are in a state of unclarity, you are always looking for an answer to keep you going. It could be in love, career, changes in your life situations or something else.

You are anxious that there is no guidance, there isn't anything that you can see, the future is unclear. If only there was some kind of clarity, a sign to tell you that you are going in the right track, it could have helped so much.

So, you are constantly looking around for that sign. Your heart yearns for an assurance, an answer.

Whatever your situation is, you need to sit and understand it wisely, you need to take your decisions based on that. Whatever numbers you are seeing, don't assign a meaning to it. It is not going to help you. What is going to help you is, you make some good use of your time to understand what you are doing, where in life you are. That will give you a clarity and if needed give you the wisdom to take the right steps. Then you are at peace, and you will not bother about these numbers.

How can I stop thinking about my Ex?

If you have had a breakup, you are going to think about that one person who was in your life and is no longer there and you both aren't together anymore in one space and time. Which means there is a big gap and so the missing is natural.

What you got to address is how are you going to fill that missing gap? What are you going to do about that big space available in your life now? It could be challenging to fill that up. But you will have to fill it up slow and steady with an understanding that it will take time to feel all fine, all good and all great.

You will have to have the understanding that it might take time, there will exist a feeling of low, something missing, not sufficient, but eventually that is going to go.

As you keep filling that hole up, which you may not be aware that you are doing a good job at, one day it will reach its brink and then you feel nothing. No more of that missing and low feeling. All of a sudden, it is like a new life has started for you.

What you need to do right now is to fill up your life with interesting aspects, those small steps. You do not have to crowd your life but engage in activities that you like. Fill your life with anything that you enjoy, even if it is meaningless to someone else, looking at your life and wondering what you are doing or why you are doing it.

Let it keep growing. Remember to keep that attention on you and be selfish to follow the path that gives you any kind of true joy.

You might feel like nothing can take the place of that person and that feeling could be really strong but in reality, if you take a step, then another step, you are going to fill up that big hole in your life with something that could grow into truly exciting.

Don't sit idle and wait and keep missing someone and thinking about the past. It is not going to do any good. You need to step up for yourself to think about how to move forward.

You need to take some decisions and learn to keep it through. It is ultra-vital.

I feel like I have lost all my confidence after the breakup. How can I regain my self-confidence?

What had completed your life for the past few years has disappeared, so you are going to feel lost because your life looks different now. A routine that you are not used to. That difference can make you feel low and less confident.

At the given state that you are in, you may have no idea how to conduct yourself after the breakup. Such a tough call and you don't even have the love and support of that person you always had in your life, who mattered in your life.

Now how are you going to take it forward? Challenging right? It is, very much. This is the tricky part, this is where people do all kinds of crazy things like stalking, spending time in meaningless activities that are remotely you, holding on to twin flames, etc. Get out of anything that makes you stuck. Anything that is going to keep you in that state of breakup and pain.

Once you start moving forward, everything around will fall in place and a new reality will emerge. Your confidence will get back on track.

How can I stop feeling the emotions and thoughts of my twin flame?

If you continue to keep believing that you are sensing and feeling everything that is going on in the heart of your twin flame, it will not be possible to stop what you are feeling. It is just going to be that way and you will have to hold on to the twin flame beliefs and ideologies to support it and to keep it that way and live the rest of your life.

What an exciting life, isn't it?

Or else, you could think and take a decision for yourself. Understand where you are, accept what has been happening in your life and decide to move forward. As long as you are not going to take a decision that helps you to look out for a better life for yourself, nothing is going to happen that will change the situation that you are in. It will only get more tense, more depressing and keep you stuck in some way or the other. Hope you understand and realise that bit.

Nothing is going to change unless you are ready to move on. If you are not ready, wait to be ready or ask the question why are you not ready? Help yourself abundantly in all possible ways to live your best life.

The book deals with this space intensively, so read again, you might get something that you missed, to get clarity over your situation.

Acceptance is a big step towards that change that your heart is seeking right now.

I do feel that sometimes there is this moment when wisdom manages to push out through all that cloud and darkness that has enveloped our inner visions and puts out a light for us. It could be such a short time, but in that time, we get this feeling of 'what am I doing?'

We get this encouragement to get out of something or see through what has been happening. If you hold on, it can reveal a lot more and help us to realise the truth. So don't ignore that light, it is there to help you.

You need that inner strength and awareness to be on the right path. If the path is wrong, how will you reach where your heart is seeking?

I do not know what direction to take after my breakup. I feel so lost.

It is called, 'change of plan'. You weren't ready for this. Maybe you knew that this relationship is not going to work out, but you still weren't ready for the breakup. Therefore, it is not going to be easy to feel all confident today and take that great step towards your best day in life.

You will have to go slow. You are going to feel bad, sad, and heavy hearted, but you can get through it.

Share what you are going through, it could be with a close friend or if you feel it is too much, ask for help through a professional who can guide you.

Sometimes we will have to lean on someone for a bit for that extra support and that is okay. That is why we are all there for each other, to help and balance and make our lives happier.

It is about you taking a step, be it asking for help or understanding that it will take time, you must move on and put yourself out there believing in the best.

I want to let go and move on, but I am unable to do it.

I want to let go.

I am unable to.

Many people fail to recognise or are never guided into having an understanding about this stage where you are in a chaotic inward journey of wanting to let go and be free and at the same time unable to do it.

Let me tell you that, this feeling of being trapped in between two opposite actions is a very specific stage of transition before you reach the realisation stage of letting go.

Do not confuse this as an inability to move past a breakup or come into a conclusion that you must hold on and stay in that relationship or breakup pain. This is purely an interim phase and sometimes one could stay on in this phase for a longer time before their mind makes that shift to move on.

Not many discuss this as a specific phase, causing people to worry and be restless. Some think that moving is a jump from break up point to the ability of moving on and when that doesn't happen, you think you will never be able to do it. And you fall into believing it and stay stuck.

Just like when you learn something new you experience this intermediate stage where you aren't so perfect and you are still learning, to get to a better level, here too it's a learning to understanding what has been happening and taking that time to be in that space and moment where you know and become aware to the better life you are going to receive by moving on, and you are happy about that decision.

Therefore, understand the importance of the transitional stage.

The moving on will happen, if you are still focussed on getting the best for you and believe it. It will happen if you are able to understand that this phase is for me to get to the next level and that the next level is going to be better.

I am not sure what that level could be for you, but it would definitely be a better phase with much more clarity to keep you going. Hence, have the trust.

How can I stop myself from reaching to my ex-partner?

I would suggest reading the pages where I have discussed about indulging more into a relationship. If you haven't got an exact closure to the relationship you had, there is a missing piece that you are trying to figure out, some communications that has not yet been done, then the tendency is that you are going to search for it.

It is vital that when you decide to take a step forward, it is a decision based on a clear understanding than, a decision that you have come up with based on some misunderstanding.

If you are seeking to reach, there is something unresolved. You need to get into that relationship with a decision to know that. It will help you to gain that clarity that will help you make the decision to stay or move on.

It is impossible for our brain to accept something that is not clarified to us, so it will always seek the answers.

Getting the answer to what your heart/brain is seeking is your next step.

It might be difficult for you to ask the person or get back into that relationship or keep the communication going because you may feel ashamed or needy. But it is important for you to know what is going on. Else even if you get into another relationship or move away, you will feel like reaching to the person and staying connected.

What you are going through here is the need to stay connected and you have to know why.

Have the courage to find that out and accept it no matter how much it hurts your ego. You may want to deny something that is not easy to accept but when you take in the reality, it allows you to move forward in your journey. It will enable the 'moving on' to happen, and as a result, you begin a new life, attracting wonderful things.

Staying on will only eventually make you feel the loss of your precious time and all the possibilities you had in that.

Can I send subliminal messages to get back my love?

Why do you want to get into such an activity? Think about all the actions that you want to indulge in with related to the love of your life. How healthy is it? What state of mind does it keep you?

Once you are inside of what you are going through, everything may seem fine. You may not be able to sense the ridiculousness of your actions or how you think.

So, if you are able to step outside and look at yourself and your life, you will realise you are putting a lot of effort into something that requires no effort at all.

All forms of love are simple, it is an indulgence of reciprocating emotions and you do not have to send subliminal messages to activate it.

If you are going to put so much effort on this one person, no matter what you do, eventually this person will slip away from your life.

Why? It is impossible for us to keep holding on to something for long. Here you are firm on your desire with a focus of never loosing this person. We can describe it as a tense state to be in. The actual joy in this state or

219

any action resulting from this state is very less. It is a tiring approach, and it can create a lot of sadness.

If you want love to manifest at its best, you need a more massive power to operate. The Universe has a special way of doing this and you should let it take over your situation than trying to send some messages out there that could backfire and be disappointing.

One of the best ways to let that power take over is by allowing the Universe to sense what you are feeling in your quietness.

Be real, be true to what you are feeling, your desires, your fears.

If you allow the Universe to sense the truth, whatever happens will be what is best for you and the person. If you both are meant to be together, it will happen with ease and it will remain in ease.

Trying subliminal messages is creating more confusion and destroying your own path. Keep life simple, allow it to manifest easily.

I am in a new relationship, but the memories of my past relationship keep coming back. How do I tackle this?

You have three factors here: you, your past, and your present. We all navigate often through our past to present and future, but it is always healthier to be in the moment and make the best of it. There is nothing like the given time, the present, with its immense energy and realness, be in it!

Now let us look at you, why do you take that trip to the memory lane? Are you missing the person? What is attracting you to the past? Observe your present, is there something missing in your current relationship or your life?

This is when you have to take the time out to understand what is happening. It would be great if you can speak about this to the person that you are with now. There would be some way that he can help you.

It could be a step to making your current relationship stronger or for you to get some clarification on your past relationship. Try to understand what it is.

Then you will know how to tackle the situation.

I feel tired and feel like giving up on my dreams most times.

Chasing can be very tiring, even when there are moments or an inner drive that you enjoy about it. The difficult bit is when things around does not happen your way and that can be disappointing and energy draining.

Putting all this together, it can diminish your energy, pull you down and exhaust you physically. It can also make you mentally stuck. If a mind is not free and happy, it cannot create and manifest.

Now, what do you do at this stage?

Take a break. It doesn't have to be for days. A day may be good enough. Eat well & sleep well. Whatever dreams that you want to make it into a reality, loosen that a bit and try to approach it differently.

Do something new.

Sometimes putting all our focus and all our hard work and sincerity can make things very stiff.

I feel you should give some space for the universe to work its way, while you go and have some fun.

During break up, what are the best ways to occupy mind's focus away from sad thoughts.

The breakup time is hard and realising this fact is important so that you can help yourself.

In all capacity, take support from your family or friends. Having their presence, love and attention is very comforting during this time. Speak in the way you feel and about what you are feeling, do not try to hide it. There is no problem in taking that time to weep out your pain or extravagantly pampering yourself to feel great. It is all okay, whatever makes you in a decent mood and gets you back to a good energy is great.

One of the best ways during this time is to rely on yourself. It means, look into yourself, ask some deep questions, find out more about you.

Take up that skill that you have always wanted to enhance but somewhere you forgot about it. Lean onto that skill or a talent that lies deep within, but you have not explored much.

Now let your mind and body work towards it. Sometimes, you may not be at a place to do anything, so give yourself more time to recover.

Remember that whenever in your life, if you are given free time, understand the value of what is given to you. There isn't anything more precious than the time that is now. It is your choice how you want to use it.

My suggestion is to engage with it in the most fruitful way. I do not mean you have to necessarily put action into that time, you could listen to music, read books, or meditate. But value it.

Do not let it pass by thinking about something that is going to spoil the rest of your day. Every moment should contribute to the next moment in such a way that you feel you are living more than 24 hours in a day.

Live a rich life!

READ AGAIN

225

* 9 7 8 0 6 4 5 2 2 7 1 0 9 *